SCAREDY CAT

Time Riddlers

For Olive & Peter

Holly Greenland & Gus Yardley
www.hollygreenland.com/books

 HGC BOOKS

Cover art & additional illustrations: Onyinye Iwu
www.onyinyeiwu.com

Proof reading: White Rose Proofreading
www.whiteroseproofreading.co.uk

To find out more about Holly Greenland, visit:
www.hollygreenland.com/books

Published by HGC Books 2023

HOW TO USE THIS BOOK

Let the adventure begin!
Can you help Alfie and Jo solve the clues on their history mystery?
Grab a pencil and paper so you're ready to go.

If you get stuck, DON'T PANIC!
Look for answers on the first page of the following chapter.
They are **<u>bold and underlined</u>**.

Good luck!

PROLOGUE
EGYPT: 1945

The archaeologist gasped as the trap door began to reveal itself beneath his trembling hands. He removed his leather hat to wipe the beads of sweat from his brow.

Reaching back for a brush, he tried again to clear the way. A gust of wind blew across his face, whipping the hot sand against his skin, gritty in his mouth and eyes. But, after many minutes carefully brushing the sand aside, his efforts were rewarded when he could finally see the entire doorway.

The five wooden planks were pinned together with thick, bronze nails. It looked well preserved. The door must have been protected by the sand, packed down tight above it for so many years.

Right in the centre was a faint row of carved Egyptian characters inside the lines of a delicate rectangle. He'd have to find out what they meant later. The man knew he should probably stop before he went any further, but he couldn't wait to see what was inside.

His heart pumped hard as he leant forward to curl his fingers around a slight crack at the side of the door, heaving with all his might. Would it budge? No; it stuck fast.

He tried again, wiggling the door from side to side. Finally, it shifted just a little. With one more almighty heave the door seemed to explode open, pushing him off his feet. He crashed backwards, then flew forwards again, as if the space inside was sucking him down.

He reached out to grab something, anything, but the sand felt like water beneath his fingers. He tipped further forward and straight through the opening that had been revealed. Now he was flying!

'AAAHHHHH!'

Deeper
Deeper
Down
Down

CRASH!

He must have been out cold for a couple of minutes at least. When he awoke, it was near darkness all around. Just a hint of light shone in from the small opening above.

There was no way he could get back up there alone.

Taking a deep breath of the stale air, the man called out as loud as he could, **'Help! Help! Anyone!'**

Finally a shadow appeared at the hole. He was saved.

'Hello? Who's down there?' the silhouette of a man in a dark hat became clear above. Instantly the archaeologist recognised the voice of his friend as it came echoing down. Thank heavens he had been working nearby.

'Light! I need a light!' he shouted back up. The

silhouette disappeared for just a minute, then returned and began lowering down an oil lamp on a long rope.

'Look out below!' came a call, the words bouncing from side to side around the underground chamber.

As the lamp came towards him, the room began to glow, and he could see further around the ancient space. Was this finally the tomb they had been searching for?

As the light flashed, swaying from side to side, he caught glimpses of the items inside. He turned in a full circle to take in the wonders. In one corner two large terracotta pots stood proud, painted in rich blues, golds and yellows. In another what looked like two large spears were leaning up against the wall, as if they had been put down just minutes before. Along the far wall, a large stone chest stood, with carvings along the side and top. What was inside? Gold, jewels?

Then, finally the man looked right into the centre of the room, where the sarcophagus of whoever was buried here stood. A carved coffin. As the light continued to swing back and forth, he could see it was painted with the sleeping face of an important person from ancient times. Their skin was golden, their headdress striped blue and black.

And then the light stopped flickering as a sound echoed around...

clink

It was a tiny noise, like two glasses striking together over Christmas dinner. The lamp had knocked something as it was travelling down towards the ground. Something that had stopped it in its tracks.

The man scrambled towards the lamp to unhook it

from the rope. Leaning in close, he could see what it had hit. Two eyes were looking at him. Two almond-shaped eyes, dark and beautiful.

He gasped as he stepped back in surprise. Only now could he see the statue in all its glory. A large black cat, shining and sleek, with a sparkling ring through its nose and two golden ears. It was standing like a lone soldier in the vast tomb, watching over the sarcophagus.

This was it. A treasure like no other.

'I've found something!' he called up, without taking his eyes off the beautiful statue.

They could make a fortune from this, surely? So why did looking into those dark, dark eyes send a shiver running down the archaeologist's spine? And why did he suddenly feel like he wasn't alone?

CHAPTER ONE

'Alfie, come down. Jo's here!'

Alfie slammed the laptop shut. His mum hated it when he did that.

'Be careful shutting that thing, we won't get another if you crack the screen!' she called up. How had she heard him from all the way down there? It was like she had ultrasonic hearing or something. He carefully reopened the laptop, just to double check it was okay. Phew. Mum had passed down her old work one for Christmas, and he loved it.

Alfie raced down, taking the stairs two at a time, then skidded along the shiny wooden floor of the hallway in his socks towards the front door. His mum hated it when he did that too.

'You'll mark the floor Alfie, how many times do I have to tell you?' she called after him.

'Sorry Mum!' he shouted back, jumping up and carefully walking the rest of the way to the front door as quickly as he could.

It was just him and his mum at the house now. Alfie's dad had died when he was small. Alfie couldn't remember much about him. Sometimes he thought he caught a smell that reminded him of his dad. Maybe it was an aftershave or his soap. And he could remember how large he'd been; a big broad man, great for hugs.

But other than that, it had been Alfie and his mum as a team as long as he could remember. She didn't like to talk about his dad, so Alfie didn't ask, and as his dad hadn't had much family either, it could feel a bit like he'd never really existed. Like maybe he was from a dream.

Before Alfie could reach the door, his mum came out of the kitchen and walked towards him. Well, more like marched. She stood straight in front of him and put a hand on each of his shoulders. Then, she pulled him in very close, her nose almost touching his, to say: 'You are to go straight to Jo's house. NO going off the cycle path, NOTHING dangerous, NO talking to strangers, and back home by five o'clock. Got it?' He nodded. There was no point arguing with his mum when she was in this mood.

'Okay, good boy,' she said slowly, before patting him on the head like a puppy and pulling him even closer for a hug.

'I'll be careful I promise. But I gotta gooooo,' whined Alfie, trying to twist away from her grasp. Urgh. She was always, ALWAYS warning him about this or that.

As he managed to escape, Alfie tried to smooth down his dark hair, ruffled from his mum's hug. Most of it sprung straight back up immediately, as it always did. Alfie had one of those faces that made him look a little cuter than he'd like. Freckled cheeks, permanently-raised eyebrows, and his ears sticking straight out on either side of his round face. His mum had called him Mouse when he was little. In fact she sometimes still did.

But Alfie was desperate to leave that nick name behind before high school came around.

'Come on slow coach!' called Jo from the front door. Jo was his oldest and best friend. His girl best friend anyway. She was brilliant. Their mums had known each other since before they were even born. She'd always been there.

Right now she was leaning against the door frame, her hair pulled back into two high bunches with yellow scrunchies, chewing on some gum. She was wearing her favourite oversized dungarees, with a spotty T shirt underneath and bright pink trainers on her feet.

Alfie never really thought about what he wore. Any old joggers and a T shirt would do him, and today was no exception. Although he had grabbed his red baseball cap before he came down, to add a bit of colour for Jo, who was now holding tight to the handlebars of her neon-green BMX. It looked massive compared to Alfie's boring old black racer, which was lying on the ground next to her.

Jo had always been tall for her age, and Alfie had always been small for his. So, although they were in the same year at school, Alfie was often mistaken for her kid brother. That could be a total pain too.

'You can't cycle with that in your mouth!' said Alfie's mum, rushing over to Jo with a tissue. 'Spit!' she demanded. Jo rolled her large eyes, which always held a slight twinkle of mischief in the corners, and spat her gum out into the tissue. 'You want to choke to death?' muttered Alfie's mum as she shook her head and walked away with her tongue sticking out in disgust.

'Sorry,' Alfie mouthed at Jo as he grabbed his shoes.

He could see the bag slung over Jo's back wheel was packed full. Fingers crossed she'd shoved some snacks in there. They always had the best food over at Jo's house.

Alfie's mum gave them a quick wave, and as she returned to the kitchen, Jo looked over and whispered, just quietly enough that his mum wouldn't hear: 'One more slide before we go?'

Alfie double checked his mum was out of sight, before following Jo back up the hallway. Side by side they took a run up to skid along the floor making it all the way to the door this time.

WEEEEEEEEE**eeeeeee**eeeeee

Jo grinned at Alfie as they came to a halt. The two giggled as they jumped up and rushed out of the door before Alfie's mum came back out.

'Ready to go?' asked Jo, already getting onto her saddle. 'I've got a good one planned today!' she whispered. Alfie felt butterflies rise in his tummy. He knew Jo had been planning this trip all week.

He looked back inside the house; nervous his mum might hear. 'Totally, I *love* going to your house!' he replied a little too loudly, with a wink to Jo. 'See you later, mum!' he called.

'Okay! And remember, FIVE O'CLOCK!' she shouted from where she was working at the kitchen side. 'Courgette and broccoli pasta bake tonight.'

'Urgh!' said Alfie quietly to Jo, who stuck out her tongue and pretended to gag, while he jumped on his own bike and reached back to slam the door.

'I heard that!' he could hear from his mum as the door closed behind him. Of course she did. See, ULTRASONIC hearing.

Jo pulled a piece of paper out of her pocket and Alfie watched as she expertly folded it into an aeroplane before stepping back to launch it over his head into the front garden behind.

'See you in five!... If you can work it out that is!' she called with a cackle before jumping onto her bike and powering away.

'Jo!!!!' called Alfie after her. But before he could even grab his handlebars, she had headed straight down the path, turned right down the road, and was disappearing out of view.

There was nothing for it, he'd have to work out whatever clue she'd left.

He scrambled to pick up the paper plane from the floor and unfolded it.

18	9	19	5	18
16	9	20	5	
16	4	5	10	16

CODE KEY

J	O		I	S		S	U	P	E	R		C	O	O	L
13	6		9	16		16	3	10	5	18		14	5	16	12
A	L	F	I	E		N	E	V	E	R					
3	12	7	9	5		1	5	19	5	18					
W	A	S	H	E	S	!		J	U	S	T				
15	3	16	17	5	16	11		13	3	16	4				
K	I	D	D	I	N	G		H	A		H	A	!		
2	9	20	20	9	1	8		17	12		17	12	11		

Hint: use the 'Code Key' to work out which number represents which letter.... here's one to get you started: 18=R.

CHAPTER TWO

Alfie squinted into the sun as he cycled down his road, and waved at the neighbours in their front gardens. There was just a whisper of wind in the air. It was only a minute or two before he turned right to head to the **River Side Steps** and began looking out for Jo. It hadn't taken him too long to crack the code, so hopefully she was still waiting.

He soon spotted her sitting with her legs dangling over the edge of the riverside, throwing pebbles into the water. She turned with a grin as she heard his wheels spinning towards her.

'Well, you took your time!' she called up, jumping to her feet and rubbing her muddy hands down her dungarees. She grabbed her bike, leapt on the saddle, and started off again, before Alfie could even pause for breath.

'Keep up!' Jo called behind her with a grin.

The flat path running beside the river was ideal for cycling. On one side was the river, and on the other were large houses with views across the water and great big gardens. Some of the houses even had their own boats moored on the riverside. The people inside must be very rich, thought Alfie. Imagine how big their tellies were!

'So what's the plan?' he asked, catching up to ride

alongside Jo.

'You know that big empty field down by Hope Farm? A load of old tyres have been dumped down there apparently and no one ever seems to check up on them. So I thought – what about climbing over the fence to build a MASSIVE obstacle course? Fastest one round wins!'

Alfie could hear his mum's words ringing in his ears. But they wouldn't do anything *dangerous*... right? Even so, his mum would only worry if she knew what they were up to. It would be best to keep today's activities to themselves. Again.

Jo was out at the front now, already racing as they rode along the path. Alfie started to push harder on his pedals to catch up. The breeze that had been so gentle as he'd left his house just minutes before was beginning to strengthen now. The wind began to force the branches overhanging the path from side to side.

One large branch let out a groaning sound as it twisted in the wind. Alfie thought how it seemed like a hand on a long thin arm reaching down to grab them as they cycled onwards. He sped up. 'Can't catch me!' called back Jo. She laughed as she turned to face forward again and lifted her bottom up off the saddle to get some extra power.

They cycled on for another ten minutes or so, as they headed further out into the countryside. Alfie would catch up one second, then fall back the next. The wind grew too, and it became harder to hear Jo as she called back every now and then to check Alfie was still following. The river seemed to run more quickly, and the leaves were flashing in the wind.

Then suddenly, a noise sounded up ahead. A cry, no, a...

SCREEEEEEEEECH!

'What was that?' Alfie called ahead, but Jo didn't seem to hear him. Within seconds, something flashed across the path in front of her.

'Careful!' shouted Alfie, as he watched Jo pull hard on her handlebars to swerve away from whatever had crossed up ahead. The front wheel of her bike made a cracking sound as it hit a stone by the path. She wobbled left and right as she tried to pull on the handlebars to steady herself, until....

CRASH!!!!

She was down in a heap at the side of the path. Her legs were folded underneath her, her arms wrapped around her head to protect her face as she fell.

Alfie pulled up next to her, his brakes screeching. 'What was that?' he called, leaning his bike on the grass, and rushing to kneel down next to her, before looking to the side to see if he could spot whatever had run across in front of them. He thought he caught a glimpse of something disappearing into the undergrowth. Was it a tail?

'I don't know what it was,' said Jo, quietly, her eyes wide. 'It was big, and black and... it was just so fast.' She was trying to understand what had happened.

'Let me get up, I'm fine,' she said, before trying to

get to her feet. But she wasn't fine. Alfie could tell that as he looked into her eyes and saw the tears come. He'd only ever seen her cry once before, when she'd bought the absolute best double sour gobstoppers from the little shop down their road, and then slipped and managed to drop them into a puddle. Disaster. They'd eaten some of them anyway mind you.

'My ankle!' cried Jo, clutching both hands around her left leg and sitting back hard on the ground. 'It hurts sooooo much...' Alfie carefully lifted the bike off her, and Jo began to frantically untie her trainer.

'AAAAAHHHHH!'

She screamed as the trainer just slightly moved her ankle joint. 'It's broken isn't it, I've broken my ankle! I'll have to go to hospital! It'll be in a cast! I won't be able to ride again!'

'Calm down, I'm sure it's not actually broken.' Alfie tried to sound calm himself, but even as he watched, Jo's ankle was beginning to swell on one side, lumpy and red. He didn't know what to do.

'Do you think you can walk back to my house?' he asked tentatively, but he knew the answer just looking into Jo's eyes. She shook her head and wiped away a tear.

Alfie looked up to see where they had stopped. Maybe there was someone nearby who could help? They had already passed all the big houses, and not so many people lived this far along the river. But he spotted that to their side was one small house standing alone. It looked pretty much abandoned. The windows were grimy, and the paintwork was peeling. It didn't look like the other fancy houses they had passed before.

'Can you see if they can help?' asked Jo pointing up to the house. Alfie hesitated. It didn't look very welcoming. His mum drove him mad. But now he wished more than anything she was here to help.

'It looks empty Jo, I don't think anyone will be there,' he said, taking a step backwards.

'No, look, the curtain, it moved,' said Jo, pointing to one of the cloudy windows on the right. Alfie froze as he watched. She was right, the curtain just slightly twitched again. Maybe someone *was* in. And perhaps they were looking out at them already.

'Oh come on scaredy cat, go and knock,' said Jo. Alfie paused again. But then she spoke more quietly, in a voice Alfie hadn't heard before. She sounded really worried. He looked down at her holding her swollen ankle, her eyes wet. 'Please, I really need help Alfie...'

Jo had no idea how hard his heart was pumping or his fingers trembling. This felt like a total role reversal. It was usually Jo who was the brave one, who would step up when it was needed. Alfie was quite happy following along. He wasn't sure he liked things this way around.

But...no one called him a scaredy cat.

'Okay, wait here,' he murmured, pulling himself up to his full height, and trying to sound confident.

'Well, it's not like I'm going anywhere, am I dumbo?!' Jo replied, and tried to give a weak smile. She hadn't lost her sense of humour at least.

Alfie went through a wrought iron gate which was propped open with a small pile of old bricks, then up the pebbled garden path to a weathered blue front door. The wind seemed to calm as he came closer to the house, the howling noise dying down with each step until it was silent.

He was surprised to find the door was open a little. He took a deep breath and knocked. It creaked a few more inches wider.

He could see that it was dark in the hallway beyond. Dark and empty. Alfie was certain now that no one was in. It must have just been the wind blowing in through the door that had moved the curtain. That was it, right?

'Ummm, hello, is anyone there?' he called, just in case.

Silence.

He was about to turn away, relieved no one was home, when a gruff voice came back: 'Do you need something, boy?'

Alfie looked back into the house, but it was still pitch black. Had he imagined it?

'Boy?' came the voice again. No, someone was definitely there.

Slowly, slowly out of the darkness an old man with scruffy grey hair, and a raggedy beard, his back hunched over a little, stepped forward into the light. His skin was wrinkly, as if it was two sizes too big for him. His old brown corduroy trousers and greying shirt could do with a wash. All in all, he looked like he might be a bit smelly.

'Ummm, yes... please,' said Alfie. His nerves were definitely showing. 'My friend, she, umm, she hurt her ankle.' He pointed behind him to indicate that someone else was nearby. It made him feel a little safer to show the stranger that he wasn't alone.

'Well, bring 'em inside then,' replied the old man beginning to turn away.

'Ummmm,' said Alfie again. Should he?

'I won't… bite,' said the old man turning back towards him, grinning a yellow, broken smile. Alfie stood perfectly still, his mum's voice ringing in his ears yet again.

Eventually, the man looked past Alfie and beckoned to Jo who had managed to stand and was now hopping through the garden gate. The decision was made.

'Hi, I've really hurt my stupid leg, can you help?' she asked. Yep, she'd always been braver than Alfie. Jo hung an arm over Alfie's shoulder and together they half hopped, half walked, in through the door.

'Thanks a lot,' said Jo, as they got their first glimpse inside the house, which was more than a little dingy and dusty.

The old man shuffled back further down the hallway and the kids followed him into a cramped living room on the right. Jo collapsed gratefully onto an old, brown armchair by the grimy window. Dust blew up as her bottom hit the cushion. It hadn't been sat in for a while.

Alfie moved over a small wooden stool for Jo to put her foot up on. He'd heard something about raising up a hurt foot, hadn't he? At least it felt like he was doing something to help.

Only once Jo was settled could he look around

the room. The walls were properly painted, although it was flaking here and there, and some damp seeped in below the window. There was at least a little fireplace with a fire burning to heat the room. Paintings covered every wall. Some bright and cheerful, others darker and creepier looking. Portraits of long-dead people looking out at them.

'Come in here, boy,' the low voice of the old man rang through the air. He must have moved to the room next door.

Alfie headed towards the voice. The door was only a crack open, and he could hear rummaging beyond. A wooden sign was nailed on the door, with just one sentence painted on it. What did it mean?

CHAPTER THREE

'**A clock**' whispered Alfie, under his breath. That must be what's inside.

He pushed the door, and held back a gasp when he revealed the small room beyond. Not just one clock, but hundreds. Clocks on every wall. There was a low rumbling sound too. The tick, tick, ticking coming from each clock. So many that it sounded like the buzzing of a bee.

There was the man, kneeling on the floor and rifling through a large case, muttering. Eventually he said, 'Hmmm, not in here,' and Alfie was sure he could hear a creak as the man unfolded himself and stood back up with a grunt. He shuffled out and into the next room. Alfie followed.

'There's a box… somewhere… full of bandages and the like. It's got a cross on it,' the old man explained. 'Keep your eyes peeled for it, would you?'

This next room was much more interesting. It was jam packed with all sorts of things lined up on shelves and stacked on the floor. Looking in from the door it seemed like a miniature ancient city with higgledy-piggledy houses and buildings in rows. Except instead of buildings, this city was made up of statues, gilded boxes, fossils and jars full of strange looking things. Each one was heavy with dust. There was just enough space in long straight roads in between the strange collections to move around.

What were they doing here? Alfie wondered. The old man must be some sort of collector.

Alfie walked over to an object that caught his eye and knelt down beside it. 'Is this a canopic jar?' he asked the old man, reaching towards the large clay pot with engravings on the outside and a crack running from the lid right to the bottom.

'DON'T TOUCH!'

The shout was so loud it made Alfie jump. 'It's valuable!' continued the old man.

Alfie stood straight back up and clasped his hands together. 'Sorry,' he said quickly. The last thing he wanted to do was anger the stranger, particularly when he was stuck inside his house.

'How do *you* know what a canopic jar is anyway?' asked the man curiously. He leant forward, then moved a few steps closer, so Alfie could almost feel his breath on his face.

'We've been learning about Egyptians at school that's all...' he explained quietly. The man was still staring at him, as if he expected him to continue, so he spoke again. 'They were so weird back then weren't they? I know they put parts of people's bodies in the canopic jars when they buried the dead. Creepy,' said Alfie.

'That's right.' The old man nodded as he leant back, seemingly satisfied with the answer. 'Except for the heart, they didn't keep that.'

The man turned away again and leant head-first into an enormous old cupboard standing in the corner of the room. It was so big he almost disappeared completely inside. 'Now where is it?'

Alfie took the opportunity to look again at the artefacts around the room. It was fascinating. He could spend hours looking at each item. If the man would let him. His eyes ran along one row until he was looking right towards the far corner of the room. There, sitting on the floor, was a large statue of a black cat. Alfie was drawn to it immediately. It was beautiful. Pitch black, like night, and so shiny it almost looked like it was glowing. In fact it was the only thing in the room not dulled by the dust.

He quietly and carefully walked along one of the roads between the items on the floor until he reached it. Standing in front of it, the cat was almost up to his shoulders. He couldn't look away from its dark eyes. He knew he shouldn't, but he wanted so much to stroke the smooth head.

Looking behind himself, he checked the old man was still riffling through the cupboard, before looking back at the cat and reaching out a hand slowly and carefully towards it. He ran his fingers across its head to pet it. The surface was cold and smooth, like a pebble on the beach turned over again and again by the waves. Then his fingers hit a long and jagged edge where an ear must have broken off.

BOOM! WHOOSH!

In an instant he felt a spark, almost like an electric shock. It ran up his arm leaving him tingling all over. It took his breath away and his eyesight blurred and flashed until all he could see was pitch black. He was sure he would faint. But he couldn't take his hand away. It was stuck fast, like super glue.

He opened his eyes. But he was somewhere else. Somewhere musty and dry, like being inside a sandy cave at the beach. He could hear faint shouting, as if someone was calling from above.

'Look out below, below, below*!'*

The words echoed in his ears and the darkness flashed with the flickering of a candle. Where was he?

Alfie blinked hard. He could see a man turning in circles as a lamp sparkled and flashed on its way down from above. Then the lamp stopped, and the man leant in to get it with a gasp.

He was looking closely at something now. Something dark and shimmering in the light. A dark and shimmering.... cat. Was it the one Alfie had been touching back in the Finds Room full of artefacts at the old man's house? But how was it here now? Alfie wanted to call out, to speak to the man. But he was scared, and when he opened his mouth his voice didn't seem to be there anymore.

'I've found something!' shouted the man.

Then he paused, and Alfie wondered if he was about to turn around and look towards him.

Alfie blinked hard again. But now when he opened his eyes it was lighter. Time had passed and the sun was streaming down from above. Shadows of people were passing overhead. The man he'd been watching was tying a large yellowing sheet around the statue, checking each corner carefully before clapping his hands to signal for it to be pulled up above.

As it rose into the air the man watched carefully from below. Alfie looked up too and saw as it reached the opening. It wobbled from side to side as the people above continued to pull.

Then a crack sounded, and something fell from above. The archaeologist tutted crossly as he watched it fall, then looked down. There, in the lamp light was one of the golden ears from the cat. It was glistening like a diamond and as smooth as a locket.

'One more heave!' came a call from above and Alfie looked back up. The cat was finally out. But what was that noise in his ears, a growl? The noise ran around the tomb, getting louder and louder.

The archaeologist opened and closed his mouth wildly, gasping for air. His eyes flickered and then shut as he began to fall to the ground.

Alfie watched, but could do nothing. Then...

BANG!

The tomb door slammed shut above them. It was pitch black again. Alfie waited for the man to shout out, or to scream. But there was nothing except for silence. Before Alfie could do anything more, he finally heard a sound.

'I SAID, DON'T TOUCH, BOY!'

It was a shout from behind him. Alfie realised his eyes were tight shut. He opened them fast and turned around.

The old man was calling out, his gruff voice booming through the air. Alfie was back in the Finds Room. He finally managed to pull his hand away from the cat, his fingers trembling.

It was like he had woken up from a strange dream.

The old man was staring at him. He looked very, very angry. His grey, watery eyes were tightly focused, and his lips pursed. Alfie let out his breath and moved his arm to cradle it with the other. His fingers were tingling and he could feel his heart bang, bang, banging in his chest.

The man was now holding an ancient looking first aid kit with a white cross on the front. He must have found it in the cupboard.

'OUT!'

The man was pointing to the door as his voice grew to a crescendo. He shuffled, faster now, back out of the room and Alfie knew he should follow.

Although before he did, he took one final look at the cat. For a split second he was sure it moved its head a little to the side. But when he looked closer, it was still. Alfie quickly followed the man out of the room and back to where Jo was waiting.

'Right, can you move it, huh?' asked the old man pointing to Jo's leg. Jo gingerly moved her ankle up and down. 'I think it may feel a little better now,' she said quietly, feeling a bit silly. The man unfurled a long length of bandage and wrapped up the ankle anyway.

'Well, this'll give ya a bit more support just in case,' he said. He turned the bandage around and around Jo's ankle until he got to the end, which he tucked in to hold it tight.

'There. Done.' The old man stood up slowly, his joints creaking as he did so.

'Thanks a lot,' said Jo standing, and carefully putting her weight on her ankle. 'Sorry we barged in on you.' She smiled sheepishly and then looked over to Alfie, who couldn't wait to get out and tell her what he'd seen.

'Yeah, thank you,' Alfie nodded. 'We better get home now though.' He rushed to help Jo back up and out of the door. As they walked away from the house towards the gate, the old man stood watching them until they hit the river path. Then he disappeared back into the darkness of the hallway and closed the door behind him.

'There was the weirdest load of stuff in the house, Jo. Jars and statues and lots of old things just piled up.' Alfie started to explain quietly, just in case the old man could hear.

'Oh yeah?' murmured Jo, distracted by her still painful ankle. As Alfie started to lift his bike, he looked back at the strange house. Then he spotted something. It was the cat statue. There it was, standing on the front porch. How on earth had it got there?

Suddenly it leapt forward with its teeth bared:

HISSSSSSSSSSS

It made him jump, but Alfie sighed with relief. It wasn't the statue after all but a real cat this time. Why was his mind playing tricks on him?

'Did you see that?' he asked Jo.

'See what?' Jo replied, getting back onto her bike, and tentatively pushing the peddle with her painful ankle, before deciding it felt just about okay to cycle home.

'Oh, never mind, let's go,' Alfie mumbled, and they rode straight back, as quick as Jo dared on her painful leg. Neither of them was in the mood for an obstacle course now.

As they turned back onto Alfie's road in silence, Jo suddenly stopped still ahead of him.

'Back!' she whispered with urgency. 'Your mum's out the front chatting with that woman from next door!'

Oh no. She would definitely know they hadn't gone to Jo's if she saw them come from this direction. And she'd be especially cross that Jo had hurt herself. She'd see it as proof positive they shouldn't be allowed out alone. No, they'd have to think of something.

'What if we cross over, go through the estate that comes out round by mine and then you can cycle back as if you were at my house all along?' asked Jo with a grin.

'Does it definitely come out by yours though?' asked Alfie, a little nervous now. He didn't know that new estate too well, it felt like a bit of a risk. The last thing he needed after the morning they'd had was to get lost.

'Well, there's only one way to find out!' said Jo, hopping off her bike and pulling it across the road as fast as her leg would let her. Alfie had no option but to follow.

They entered the maze-like paths through the rows of cookie-cutter houses looking for the exit out the other side to Jo's road. Would they make it through from the river to her house?

CHAPTER FOUR

Yes! They had made it out of the estate and back home without any suspicions from his mum – phew!

Alfie hoped that would be the end of it. That the house and the cat would just be a strange encounter he could now forget. But days later, Alfie still couldn't stop thinking about that statue. It really had seemed to glow. And what had happened when he touched it?

The next Saturday Jo was off at a football tournament all day. She wouldn't be able to play with her ankle still recovering, but her loud voice made her a great supporter from the side-lines. That meant it was just Alfie and his mum at home. Alfie was keeping himself busy while she caught up on work. Boring. So when she came into his room zipping up her coat, Alfie was hoping for something exciting to do. 'I'm dropping some books back at the library, do you want to walk into town with me?' she asked.

'Urgh,' said Alfie under his breath. This wasn't what he'd been hoping for.

'We could grab a muffin at the vegan café after?' she said. As if *that* was a treat. He was about to protest when he had an idea. The library! He'd had a book out ages ago for school and it said something that might be useful. He could only half remember it; it hadn't seemed important at the time, but now it was.

'That sounds great mum, let me get my shoes on!' he called, rushing past her and down the stairs. She smiled after him, pleased he was so excited to go out with her for the morning. She had no idea that he had his own plans for their library trip.

Once inside the library, Alfie's mum went to the main desk to drop back in her stack of mystery books she always read before bed, while Alfie went to the history section. He ran his hand along the spines of each book. Purple, blue, yellow. Most were thick, with hard covers. All were full of facts. He muttered the names under his breath as his hand hit each book: 'Viking Hats: A History,' 'The Drainage Systems of Ancient Rome', 'The Sounds and Smells of Medieval England.'

Then he stopped: 'Mysteries of Egypt'. This was it. He grabbed the book and turned straight to the back where an index told him which page to go to for each topic.

'Aha!' he exclaimed, as he spotted what he was looking for: 'Cats: p.19, p.25, p.32'.

He flicked first to page 19. It had a picture of a tile with a faded jewelled cat painted onto it. A label underneath said it was illegal to take a cat out of Egypt. There was an actual law against it! Interesting, but not the fact he was looking for.

Over to page 25. Apparently they loved cats so much that their enemies would put cats on their shields so the Egyptians wouldn't fight them. Wow! But that wasn't what he wanted either.

The final page - 32. Yes! Here it was:

Cats were important animals to ancient Egyptians, representing power. They were admired for killing venomous snakes and were thought to protect the pharaoh in life and in death.

Alfie knew that the pharaoh was the most important person in Egypt, so cats must have been thought of as very powerful.

He read on. The page said that lots of people were buried with cat statues and even mummified dead cats (yuck). It was thought they would go with them to the afterlife. That was where Egyptians thought they went after they died.

So how had one ended up at that old man's house?

He picked up the book and took it out to read more later.

That night he didn't sleep well. His dreams were full of cats hissing and screeching at him, and he tossed and turned all night. His final nightmare began on another bike ride. But this time it was just him, no Jo for protection. It was dark and he had stopped his bike outside an old empty building. It was raining hard, and he went inside to shelter. The rain was pounding on the metal roof:

Rat-atat- atat!

He looked about him. There were mirrors hanging from every wall. He spun around but all he could see was himself, from every angle, flashing in the mirrors.

There was no one else there, but it was like he could feel someone watching him. Or some*thing*. He turned to leave, but the door he'd entered through had disappeared. It was just a blank wall now, with yet another mirror hanging from it. Just Alfie looking back at himself.

He began desperately searching for the exit, spinning in circles. But there was no door, no window, nothing. He stopped spinning to take a breath and make a plan. From the corner of his eye, he thought he saw something move.

Alfie spun around as quickly as he could. There it was. A large cat walking slowly and stealthily towards him. Its eyes were staring straight at him, its dark fur was sticking up on end, its long tail pointing into the air. It was larger than an average cat. In fact, it looked like the black cat statue from the old house come to life.

He tried to run, but his feet wouldn't move. It was useless anyway. Where would he go? He was trapped.

Then he spotted it. Behind the cat there was now a doorway. The door was just open enough that Alfie could see through to the outside. There was a bright green field, dotted with flowers, and a clear blue sky. That's where he needed to go to escape! But between him and the door was the black cat, and it didn't look like it would let him pass. The cat had stopped now, and was sitting bolt upright in the exact same pose as the statue.

It tilted its head to the side. Then it stood up and lifted one giant paw to rub across its ears before placing it back down to the ground. Alfie watched in silence as the cat then turned away from him to face the doorway.

It began to walk; slow, sleek steps. Then it paused and looked back at Alfie before turning and walking again. Was it asking him to follow?

Alfie tried again to lift his feet to take a step forward. He so wanted to know where the cat was going. But he was afraid, too. His heart was pumping fast, the noise of it pounding in his ears.

Finally his feet released, and he felt as if he was lifting right up off the floor. He was floating after the cat, moving through the air like a leaf on the wind. He looked towards the door, and could see now, as he got closer, that a sign was hanging on it. What did it say?

He twisted and turned but he couldn't get a good view of it. Then he remembered… the mirrors! He looked to the mirror facing the door and could see the sign. Of course the word was reflected. He squinted his eyes to get a better look, but before he could work out what it meant, his eyes flicked open, and he could see his messy old bedroom….

'ALFIE, I WON'T CALL AGAIN, TIME TO GET UP!'

It was the voice of his mum echoing up from downstairs.

As he shook himself awake, he sat bolt upright and could feel beads of sweat on his forehead and dripping down the back of his neck, tickling his skin. He let out a sigh and dropped his head back on his pillow.

'I said, you're going to be late for school, come down for breakfast…please!' he heard. He screwed his eyes tight shut again and tried hard to remember the reflection he'd seen of the sign on the door.

He could picture it. Now he just needed to flick it around in his mind.

Or if he held it up to a mirror, might that work?

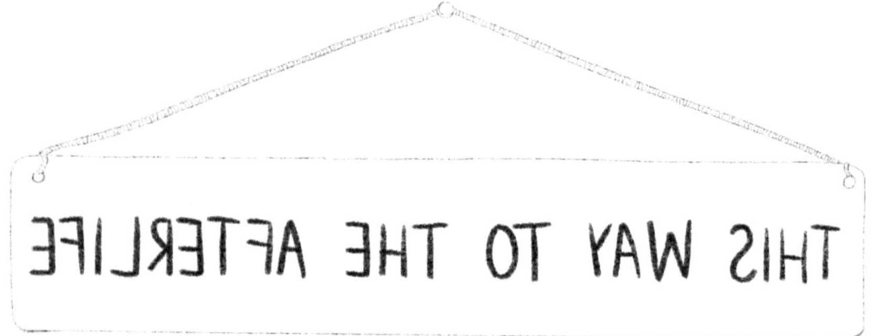

CHAPTER FIVE

School was tough that day. Alfie felt like he'd hardly slept at all and seemed to be yawning every few minutes. All he could think about was that strange dream and the door with its mysterious sign – **<u>'This way to the afterlife'</u>** it had said. What did it mean?

At break, he found his friend Rex in the playground. They knew each other from swimming. Rex was lucky to be in Miss Brook's class, while Alfie was with Mr Grim who was super strict. But they sometimes bumped into each other at break and lunch.

As usual, Rex was surrounded by a big gaggle of friends near the basketball hoops. Alfie didn't play basketball. And he didn't have a million friends like some of the kids at school. He didn't mind though, he quite liked spending time by himself. But today he needed someone.

He pulled Rex by the arm and led him over to the upside-down tree round the back of the outdoor games shed. It grew with its branches bent over, its cascading leaves creating a den inside. Alfie often hid out here at break. 'Come here quick, I've got to tell you something,' he called to Rex.

'This better be good, Alfie,' Rex replied as they got to the tree. He crouched on the ground, not wanting to sit down and get his uniform dirty. He always looked immaculate. Neatly ironed shirt, clean jumper, shiny shoes. The opposite of Alfie, who was happy if he made it to school without odd socks on most days.

Alfie told Rex all about the strange dream he'd had, finishing with the major drama: '...then my feet began to lift off the ground and it was like I was going to float after the cat and out the door! And there was this weird sign, that said outside led to.... The Afterlife!'

He leant in close, waiting for his friend's reaction. He thought he'd be shocked, maybe even gasp, but Rex just rolled his eyes.

'It's a dream Alfie, dreams are always weird aren't they? I once had a dream where I was half boy, half crocodile and I came into school and ate the teachers. And then all the kids cheered, and we had a massive birthday cake in the hall before we went home early.' His eyes drifted away for a second. 'That was the best dream ever,' he said, looking into the distance.

Then he shook his head and turned back to Alfie. 'Can't believe you dragged me out under this muddy old tree for this one, it's rubbish!' He started to get up to return to his friends.

'But, but... the cat looked like it wanted me to follow it. What if it needs my help?' asked Alfie.

Rex pushed the branches aside as he headed out from under the tree and then glanced back. 'You're crazy Alfie Green. Just forget about it, okay?' He shook his head and Alfie watched as he walked back across the field, his hands jammed into his trouser pockets.

Perhaps Rex was right. It was just a dream after

all. And he must have imagined what happened at the house. What was so special about him that an ancient cat would be trying to communicate with him? He was just boring old Alfie. It must all be in his head.

As the bell went to signal the end of break, Alfie jumped up and ran back across the field to make it in time for class. He didn't want to get on the wrong side of Mr Grim.

As he rushed to his seat, he could see paper and pencils laid out on each of the tables. Mr Grim explained, with his typical grumpy look on his round pink face, that in today's lesson they would be finishing off their topic about myths and legends.

'The lesson notes say this activity should be...,' he paused, before saying with a grimace, 'fun.' He shivered a little, as if he hated the word.

'Before we start, can anybody tell us about one of the legends we've been learning about?' The teacher's voice boomed across the room.

Alfie knew exactly what he wanted to say. He wanted to tell the class all about the importance of Egyptian cats. But he'd promised himself to forget all about that for now, so he kept his hand down.

'Nobody?' asked Mr Grim, shaking his head. 'You are a useless bunch!' he snarled, looking round the room. Alfie was sure people had lots of ideas, but no one wanted to speak up in Mr Grim's class, not if they weren't 100% sure of their answer.

'Well, get on with it then. Turn over your work sheet. Find the myths and keep quiet,' called Mr Grim. Everyone turned over their paper while their teacher sat at the desk and brought out a newspaper to flick through.

Alfie looked down. A wordsearch. Good, he quite enjoyed these.

He picked up his pencil and tried to find the first word, but his brain wouldn't let him focus. The letters floated in front of his eyes, and the words just wouldn't appear. His mind was somewhere else.

'Hmmm, not found even one Alfie?' came the whiny voice of Mr Grim from over his shoulder. He must have got up to patrol the room. 'Time is a-ticking!' he said, with a weaselly grin as he tapped his watch with his finger.

Alfie looked back down, desperately searching. Nothing. He decided to write his name in the corner, as if he'd found a word. Maybe that would keep Mr Grim off his back for a few minutes. He picked back up his pencil and tried to shape the letters. But, **SNAP,** the tip of the pencil broke beneath his hand. Typical. Alfie tutted and stood up to go to the table by the window where the big electric sharpener was attached to the wall.

As he slipped his pencil into the sharpener, his mind wandered, and he looked out of the window in front of him. His classroom was one floor up and he had a good view over the whole of the school field from here.

There, to the left, was the upside-down tree he loved so much. He wished he could go back out there and hide right now. Escape Mr Grim. Maybe even have a little nap!

He looked up to the sky. What a horrible day it had turned into. It had been clear and blue at break time, but now the sky was dark and gloomy. Grey clouds were slowly shuffling across the sky and blocking out the sun. It looked like it might rain at any moment. He'd probably get soaked later walking home.

Then he looked back down to the tree.

His.
Heart.
Stopped.

There, in amongst the bowed branches, were at least twenty cats, all sitting as motionless as statues and all staring up at HIM.

He stood stock still, staring back. Was he dreaming again? Keeping his eyes firmly on the cats, he took his pencil out of the sharpener and stabbed the now pointed end into the back of his other hand.

'Ouch!' Nope, definitely not asleep.

What should he do? He turned to Mr Grim, who was standing at a table nearby telling Sophie she wouldn't amount to anything. His favourite conversation.

'Mr Grim,' he tried to call, but his voice came out as a quiet whisper.

He looked back out of the window. Yep, they were still there. Black cats, tabby cats, ginger cats. All standing perfectly still, and all looking up at him. Alfie wanted to open the window, to shout outside and scare them away. But he knew he'd get in deep trouble if he did.

Clatter, clatter, clatter... came a noise right next to him. It took a second before he realised he'd dropped the pencil he'd been holding. It had fallen to the floor, hitting the table on the way down.

'What's all the noise?' said Mr Grim from right behind him now.

'Sorry, it's just that… that… well, take a look for yourself.' Alfie stepped back, pointing with a shaky hand out of the window.

He watched his teacher's face closely as he leant forward to get a better view outside. He was expecting him to shout in surprise, or to scream in terror, but he simply said in an exasperated voice: 'What is it? There's nothing there. Nothing!'

Alfie looked back out.

Where a whole pack of cats had been standing just seconds before, there was now nothing. The field, and the tree, looked completely normal. Even the clouds had cleared, and the sun was shining down onto the school as if nothing had happened at all.

He was shaking his head now in disbelief. Where had they gone?

He looked at Mr Grim, his mouth hanging open, not sure what to say. 'I, I, I, I thought I saw something…' he said quietly before his voice trailed off.

'What?' leant in Mr Grim, his eyes narrowed. 'Speak up!' he shouted.

Alfie thought about trying to explain. But what would he say? 'I saw a load of cats, creepy cats, in the field and I think it's because of this old statue I touched, and I think they want something from me…'. No, then he'd really think Alfie had lost it.

'Back to your seat now Green! No more time

wasting!' came his teacher's booming voice, his short, stubby arm pointing towards Alfie's desk.

'And you aren't going until you've completed the worksheet. Got it?'

Well he'd just have to finish it as quickly as possible so he could get home, wouldn't he? thought Alfie. Eight words to find, he could do it.

But what was that?

Two other words jumped out together, starting with the letter B. Right there in the puzzle, where they shouldn't be! They weren't on the list Mr Grim had given them... why were they there?

F J U V M S L G E J R R Z K U

L Q Y P T O N F H R X F N Q S

O L V L W I T C H O I V Q S L

W T A C K C A L B W S P V P X

E L Z G Q U N H A L L T M V N

R X T X T C I M N K D C Z A X

E Q E D X M E T Y P W Z S V V

W K F C H R O F P L W W P H C

H L O G M I M A L I T E Y X E

E J Z A W S F I N T F Y Z D I

M R I S Y G Q R M I P R X T G

T D E H F P J Y P Q R U V J J

I Q A T X H G B V R B E G Q P

C O X E I F L F K C Z A R Q Y

R G E Q H E Y Q M S H J Z I M

Yeti	Elf	Mermaid	Vampire
Ghost	Witch	Werewolf	Fairy

Hint: if you get stuck, you can find the eight answers and the surprise word revealed on the 'Crossword Answers' page at the end of this book.

CHAPTER SIX

The **<u>Black Cat</u>** had been following him in his dreams, and now into his schoolwork too. How had those two words got there? Two ordinary words that would have meant nothing to Alfie just a few days ago, and now filled him with dread.

After showing Mr Grim he'd completed the puzzle, Alfie sat quietly and kept his head down until the final bell went, before rushing as quickly as he could out the gates and back home.

It was usually a five-minute walk back to his house, but today he did it in three. His mind was whirring. Could he really have seen all those cats outside? And why had those exact words appeared in his class work? He wanted to talk it through with someone, to get a second opinion. But he knew his mum wouldn't understand. Or perhaps she would, and she'd completely FREAK out.

It was times like this he wished his dad was still around. Perhaps he'd have had a theory, or at least want to join him on an adventure to find out. But he wasn't here, so that was that.

But... maybe there was one person who he might just be able to convince.

Alfie hid away in his room until teatime, waiting until the right moment to escape. Then after dinner, when he knew his mum would want to sit down quietly to watch her programme, he grabbed his helmet and ran towards the front door.

'Wait!' came a shout behind him as his mum's head appeared around the living room doorway.

'And where are you going?' she asked.

'Just over to Jo's. I want to talk to her about… ummm… something from school.'

'I'll walk over with you then,' his mum replied, coming into the hallway, and already starting to look for her shoes.

'No mum, I'll be fine. I don't even need to cross a road. You don't need to take me anymore.'

She sighed. 'Okay, I know, you're growing up. Just… be careful okay?'

'I promise!' he called as he bolted out the door before she changed her mind.

'Stay on the pavement!' he could hear her voice still calling as he jumped on his bike.

In just a couple of minutes he was at Jo's house. It was similar to Alfie's from the front. Built of brick, two floors, two windows, and one front door. But it felt completely different. Whereas Alfie's was always super neat and tidy, even from the front door you could see Jo's was not. Outside on the mat was a pile of grubby welly boots from Jo and her twin big brothers, Benji and Sam. And even once the door opened, the bright, stripy welcome mat was caked in mud from mucky feet arriving home after their adventures. Down the hallway the carpet was dotted here and there with splashes of pink squash, brown chocolate crumbs and little piles of acorns picked up from the park. It was great!

'Are we meant to be meeting tonight?' asked Jo, looking a little confused as she opened the door. She had a big bag of cheese puffs in her hands, and she licked the orange dust off her fingers while she waited for a reply.

'No, not tonight. But something weird is going on and I think I need your help,' Alfie explained.

Jo had been planning a movie marathon with her brothers, but she could see Alfie was really serious. This was too intriguing to turn down. She rushed inside to explain to her dad she was going out. Alfie could hear him murmur a quick response before she ran back to the front door and pulled on her trusty old trainers. Within seconds she was outside on her bike and Alfie was leading them back down to the river.

'Where are we going?' asked Jo. 'Oh, are we finally going to do my obstacle course?'

'Afraid not,' replied Alfie. 'Something strange has been going on and I need to get to the bottom of it.'

As they cycled, he told Jo the whole thing from the start. How he'd felt a strange spark when he'd touched the statue; seeing the hissing cat on the porch that had felt almost like a warning; the bad dream he'd had; the cats he'd seen out on the field that had disappeared; and finally the words *Black Cat* appearing in his schoolwork.

'I don't know what it means, but I know it's all tied up with that old man's creepy house and the statue I touched there,' finished Alfie.

Jo cycled silently. All Alfie could hear was her wheels as they clicked around, like the ticking of a clock.

Tick   Tick   Tick   Tick

'Well, what do you think?' asked Alfie, finally, not able to wait any longer.

'I think you've gone totally bat crazy, and made me miss my movie marathon,' Jo replied. She stopped her bike right where she was, ready to turn around. Alfie was disappointed; she was looking at him with the same expression as Rex earlier. Maybe he was crazy after all. He tried one more time.

'I know it sounds mad. But I promise you, it's been happening,' he pleaded. 'And I have a really bad feeling about it. The only thing I can think is that we go back to the house and find out if the old man knows anything more about that statue.' He looked at Jo, willing her to trust him.

'I want to believe you,' said Jo, looking unsure. 'But, come on, nightmares, cat gangs – all just a coincidence, surely?' she asked.

'I mean, look. There's a cat right now, should I be scared?' Jo laughed as she pointed at a large tabby cat sitting by the river.

'Oooooh, creepy cat, don't attack me! Gosh Alfie, you really are a scaredy cat sometimes,' she held up her hands and laughed again. 'Ahhh! There's another one. Maybe it's coming to get us!' she called as she pointed at a bench nearby where a black cat was sitting licking its paw. Alfie felt anger rise in his tummy.

But there was a pause, and when Jo spoke again, this time her voice was quieter and she wasn't laughing now. 'There's another one…' she said, pointing behind Alfie. He looked back too and saw another large grey cat walking slowly towards them. Then behind the large grey, coming from further down the path, he could see another. Two, three, four, maybe TEN cats were now walking up to join them. The furthest one away started to speed up and soon a whole tribe of cats was running their way.

'Okay, Okay, I believe you!' whispered Jo, her eyes wide. She jumped back on her bike and shouted as loud as she could: 'Quick, let's get out of here!'

They both started to cycle fast up the path, pumping their legs to gather speed. Once he thought they might be far enough ahead, Alfie looked behind him. Now a whole army of cats was following them, their long slender legs leaping forward. It forced the friends further onwards.

'We're nearly at the old house,' he said eventually, breathing hard. Finally they reached the spot where Jo had hurt her ankle the week before. They leapt off their bikes, dumped them on the grass, and raced up the path to the door of the old man's house.

It opened before they even knocked.

'I wondered if you'd be back, get inside, quick!' said the old man, opening the door just wide enough to get them through, and then slamming it behind them.

BANG!

They were back inside the dusty old house, and the man led them quickly into the living room. Alfie shivered as he watched the light from the window dance around the room as the curtains moved in the breeze, creating shapes, and playing with his mind.

Stars flashed before Alfie's eyes, and he blinked

hard to clear them. An image was breaking into bits before him, like jigsaw pieces thrown up in the air.
Could he work out which pieces fit where?

Hint: match the numbered pieces to the stars labelled with letters.

CHAPTER SEVEN

The man quickly pulled the curtains tight closed at the windows and the stars stopped swirling in front of Alfie's eyes. He blinked hard, and could now picture the full outline of the cat that he was sure was waiting just outside (**A1, B5, C6, D3, E4, F2**). He imagined it tearing at the glass with its long, sharp claws.

There was just one old light turned on now, hanging low in the centre of the room. It flickered slightly as the man paced.

'What's going on?' asked Alfie in shock.

The man spun around to look at the kids, his eyes sparkling. He wasn't shuffling like last time. In fact he seemed buzzing with energy. 'I knew you'd been brought here for a reason,' he was saying, as he walked up and down.

'But… what reason?' asked Alfie, shaking his head. He was desperate to know.

'Look, sir, we've just been chased here by an army of cats,' said Jo, taking charge. 'I think you need to explain to us right now what is going on!' She was never one for beating around the bush.

The man stopped pacing and turned to look at them. He stood, thoughtful for a few seconds, before speaking again. 'Okay,' he said quietly, sitting down in one of the old armchairs. His faced had softened and his eyes cooled.

'Firstly, enough with the "sir". I'm Raymond. You can call me Ray, okay?' he gave a half smile as the children nodded.

'So, I think something strange happened when you were last here, didn't it?' asked Ray, turning to Alfie. 'When you touched something you shouldn't have touched. Is that right, young man?'

Alfie looked down. 'Yes, I'm sorry. It was when I touched the cat statue. It felt… well, it felt very strange,' he explained. Ray nodded, but said nothing.

'It was like it was alive, or electric, or something. I'd never felt anything like it!' Alfie shook his head. 'And for just a second or two it was like I was somewhere else entirely. Where did it come from? Do you know?' he asked.

'Wait here,' replied Ray, leaving the room. Alfie and Jo looked at each other. Jo raised her eyebrows and crossed her eyes trying to lighten the mood. She always did that when she was freaked out by something. But this time Alfie couldn't smile.

When he returned, Ray was wiping the dust off a black and white photo with the back of his hand. He passed it to Alfie and Jo who held it between them and looked closely.

There were two men in the picture, perhaps around thirty years old. They were smiling, with an arm around each other. They were sitting on old canvas chairs wearing suits, even though it looked like they were in the desert. They must have been boiling! One of the men was wearing a light-coloured brown hat, the other a hat made of black leather. Next to them, two large shovels lay on the floor.

'Are they archaeologists?' asked Jo. She'd seen pictures like this at the museum in town.

'Yes. The one on the right, with the black hat, is my grandfather. He was called Peter Murrey. The one on the left is his best friend and dig partner, Charlie Green.'

'Green. But that's my last name, isn't it Jo?!' exclaimed Alfie, shocked.

'Aha…' Ray smiled. 'So you are connected to the cat, just like me!' he declared.

'Maybe he was my…. grandfather?' asked Charlie.

'No, I don't think so,' Ray shook his head. 'Not old enough my boy. But perhaps he's your *great grandfather*? That would work!' Ray looked excited now. 'Have you heard about Charlie Green from your parents at all?' he asked.

Alfie shook his head. 'This would be my dad's grandfather I guess, but …' Alfie's voice faltered as he wondered if he should tell the old man his dad was gone. Before he could decide, Ray spoke again. 'That means you're his direct descendent.' His smile broadened, like he'd solved the biggest mystery in the world. 'I knew I could feel a spark in the air between you and that old statue as soon as you entered my Finds Room.'

'I've tried to sell that darn thing so many times, but it's always fallen through or been returned. It's like he wanted to stay here. So I've just left him there, sitting in the corner, keeping my distance. Letting it stay for whatever it was it was waiting for.' Ray shook his head, then leaned in close. 'And listen here. I think all this time that cat has been waiting… for *you*.'

'But what does it want from *me*?' asked Alfie quietly. His heart was beating faster now.

'I'm not sure… but we need to find out, and quickly,' said Ray. 'What do you know of your great grandfather?'

'Nothing. I'd not even heard of him before now. I didn't know my dad… and my mum doesn't like to talk about him or his family back at home…' Alfie's voice trailed off. He'd always known he'd missed out on his dad. But never thought much about the wider family he'd missed out on too. A whole history he had, that he didn't know anything about.

'Not to worry, I may have something that can help. I found the photograph stored with a letter from my grandfather. Let me get it for you.'

After several minutes, Ray returned with a browned piece of paper with faded writing on it. Alfie and Jo waited patiently as he unfolded it gently and scanned down the letter and then nodded. 'Here we are,' he said, before starting to read out a section from it:

I will be returning straight away from Egypt.

On Monday we finally found the tomb we had been searching for. But something happened to poor Charlie. As we removed an artefact, the tomb door slammed shut and jammed.

For many hours we couldn't get it open, no matter how hard we pulled. It was stuck. When it finally opened later that night, there was no sign of Charlie anywhere. His bag was lying on the floor open, but otherwise there was nothing to show he'd ever been in there at all.

Ray looked up. Jo was sitting open-mouthed in shock. Alfie's eyebrows were raised higher than they'd ever gone before. He was trying to make sense of what he was hearing. The old man continued:

When it was morning I went down into the tomb in the light. I walked all the walls, but there were no doors or secret passageways. Just no way he could get out. Not even a sign of a slip or a fall, nothing.

We decided to leave as soon as we could and not touch any more in the tomb. So all we have to show for our journey is the large black cat statue Charlie had found, just a little damaged. I have sent it home ahead of us, and we must keep it as a memory of Charlie. Maybe he will turn up again someday.

'And that's how the statue ended up in your house!' said Jo, starting to understand what had happened. Ray nodded.

'What do we do now?' asked Alfie, bewildered, looking over to Jo.

Jo got up and went to the window, drawing back the curtains. 'Well, the coast is clear. Why don't we go back to your house and ask your mum if she knows anything about your great grandfather?'

Alfie nodded, although he was pretty sure she wouldn't know a thing or even want to tell him if she did. They thanked Ray again and promised to return if they found out anything that could help them solve the mystery.

As they headed out of the door again, Ray called after them. 'Wait, take this with you, it may be useful,' and he handed Alfie the old photo.

'Thank you,' he replied, reaching for it. He was grateful to take it with him, this could perhaps be the only photo of his great grandfather in existence.

As they walked down the path, he turned the photo over, and on the back found a handwritten note in neat, curling letters, reading –

Peter & Charlie 1945

The greatest SHIP t'was ever made is light as any feather,

It keeps us safe and grows with time so long as we're together.

Hint: this ship doesn't float on the water...

CHAPTER EIGHT

Alfie smiled as he jumped onto his bike. A great "ship" that always grows if you're together. A **FriendSHIP**. It must be. The two men had obviously had a great partnership. How sad it had been cut short in such a mysterious way.

Alfie and Jo rode back as fast as they could, their legs pumping and wheels turning with such speed, you could hardly see the spokes as they flew round and round.

In no time they were at Alfie's front door on Albion Road, breathing hard. Alfie's mum opened up with a smile across her face. But immediately the smile dropped. She could see something was wrong.

'What's happened, are you all right? Something's happened hasn't it?' she asked, worried. She was looking them up and down like she might be able to spot a broken bone.

'We'll explain everything soon mum,' Alfie said, rushing into the house with Jo not far behind.

'Can you come in here please Mrs Green; we need to ask you some questions. It's important,' called Jo, as she took a seat on the sofa with Alfie.

Alfie's mum entered the room behind them. She still looked completely bewildered. But she took a seat and then a deep breath. She was preparing herself for bad news. Jo looked to Alfie, and gave a reassuring nod so he would speak.

'We have a question for you, but… I don't want you to get upset or…well, you don't have to answer it if you don't want to, okay?' said Alfie to his mum, who was looking more confused than ever now.

'Put me out of my misery kids, what is it?' she looked over to Jo who, true to form, blurted straight out with it. 'We need to know about Alfie's great grandfather, Charlie Green. Do you know anything about him?' she asked.

Alfie's mum's shoulders dropped as she relaxed. 'Is that all you were going to ask me? I thought something terrible had happened!' she said, a smile spreading across her face. Alfie was shocked; she didn't look sad at all.

'No, that's all Mum. I know you don't like to talk about them much, but we'd really like to know,' said Alfie quietly.

'Of course. You only ever have to say if you want to talk about your dad, or his family, or anything. I never want to rush you, but I'm here for any questions, okay?' she said, a soft smile spreading across her face. So, *she* had been waiting for *him*?

'But, why do you ask?' his mum continued.

'It's for a… for a…' Alfie couldn't think of a good excuse. His mind had gone blank.

'It's for the school project we're working on,' said Jo, saving Alfie at the last second.

'That's it, the school project!' agreed Alfie, smiling. Perfect!

'Well, okay, let me see. I never met him myself of course, and neither did your dad. But he used to tell stories about him that had been passed down through the family. I remember he was an interesting character. I know he travelled a lot and loved exploring. In fact there was a family legend that he'd gone missing on one trip to Egypt, not long after your dad's dad… so *your* grandad, had been born,' she explained. Alfie looked round at Jo and nodded. That confirmed it, the missing man *was* his great grandad.

'But that's about all I know I'm afraid,' his mum finished. Jo sighed and looked back over at Alfie. That didn't really help much.

'We might have a box of his things up in the loft now I think of it. They came to us after your gran-gran passed away and I doubt your dad moved them out. I haven't been up there in so long. But there may be some bits you can use for your project. It's probably all rubbish. Do you want me to get it down?' she asked.

How had Alfie not known about this before? He knew barely anything of his dad's family, and now there was a box of stuff?! He could hardly hide his excitement.

'Yes, yes, yes! Now!' shouted Alfie.

'Pardon me?' his mum replied, shocked.

'I mean, yes please mum!' he said again, in his most polite voice.

She was gone for what seemed like forever, digging around in the dusty old loft. The floorboards creaked and cracked above the kids' heads as they waited. After about twenty minutes Alfie started to give up hope as the banging quietened from above them and they could hear his mum start to climb back down the ladder.

'There's loads up there,' she was saying with a

smile. 'I'd packed it away so long ago; I'd hardly remembered what we had. We'll have to get it all down soon Alfie.' She ruffled his hair as she walked past him back into the room. Boxes of stuff about his dad and his family? Alfie didn't know what to think of that. But it would have to wait while he solved this first mystery.

'This is the one I think you want. Here.' Alfie's mum put one plain brown box down. On the side it had large black writing saying: 'Grandad Charlie's stuff'.

Alfie looked at Jo. Jo looked at Alfie. This could hold the answers they were looking for.

Jo was the first to lean in to look. Alfie felt he needed just a second to prepare himself. This was a connection right back to his past. Epic.

Finally, he leant in to see. Inside the old cardboard box was another box. This one looked even older. Jo reached in and took one side. 'Give me a hand,' she said to Alfie, who took the other. They lifted it out and laid it on the floor. This box was more like a wooden crate, stamped with information in a foreign language.

'Wow,' murmured Alfie quietly. It was like finding treasure.

'I'll leave you to it, okay?' asked Alfie's mum, her hand on his shoulder. He nodded as she left the room quietly.

'His things sent back from Egypt do you think?' Jo asked Alfie, once his mum was out of the room.

'Maybe. Let's open it,' Alfie replied.

They used a pen, tucked under the lid to lever it off. As they opened it up a whisper of a **creeeeeeaaaaaaaaaaaaaak** sounded. Dust burst into the air and seemed to glisten in the sun which shone in from the window. It fell like golden rain, and beams of light landed right inside the box as the lid leant backwards on the floor.

Alfie bent over to look inside.

'What's in there?' asked Jo quietly.

'Just an old bag.' Alfie shook his head, disappointed.

He reached in and picked out the bag. It was made of canvas with leather straps and buckles. It felt empty when he lifted it. Jo took it from him and put it carefully onto the rug. She began to look through the bag and the pockets around the outside. Each time she opened a pocket she shook her head.

'You're right, nothing,' she said, not trying to hide her disappointment.

They sat quietly.

'What now?' she asked Alfie.

Alfie shrugged his shoulders and picked up the bag to put it back into the crate. As he lifted it, a piece of paper fluttered down onto the floor. Perhaps it had been caught underneath. It was folded up. It opened as it landed, like a butterfly.

'Aha!' declared Jo, picking it up. 'Looks like a receipt or something. But it's handwritten. Must be pretty old.'

Alfie took the paper from her and looked closely at the writing. It was hard to make out. There was a date in the first line. 'Does that say 1st July 1945?' he asked Jo, who leant in and nodded in agreement.

'Then below it says something like, 'One Egyptian Artefact''. He looked closely and two more words were written beneath. These were the most faded of all.

'Snail Cup?,' read Alfie. 'That doesn't make any

sense. What's a snail cup, and why would you buy one?'

Jo grabbed the paper off Alfie and looked again. "Small cup' you dope! It says, 'Small Cup!' And a number – 1184.'

'Okay, okay,' said Alfie, crossing his arms. 'So, someone bought one small Egyptian cup and put the receipt safely in my great grandad's empty old bag and then sent it on to my family? Why would they do that?' Alfie was baffled.

'I don't think this is a receipt to show they *bought* something. I think it's a receipt to prove they *lent* it to someone,' explained Jo. 'Look here, right at the top it says: "County Museum, Loan's Department."' She leant over to Alfie and pointed to the faded stamp at the top of the paper.

'Right. So at some time after the bag came back, the cup was lent to the County Museum,' said Alfie, trying to understand what had happened, 'and… and I guess it could still be there? Right?' he asked excitedly, looking at Jo for confirmation.

'I guess so,' she replied, her curls bobbing as she spoke.

'Then, we need to go there and see if we can get whatever it is!' said Alfie.

'But your mum would never let us go to the museum alone!' said Jo.

'No, I wouldn't,' came a voice from behind them. Alfie's mum had obviously not been far away. 'You want to go to the museum?' she asked, looking surprised.

'Yeah for the… the project we told you about,' explained Alfie, sticking to his story.

'Okay. Well if it's for school, I can jump on the bus with you. But we'll need to be quick. Come on!' The two kids leaped up, and Alfie tucked the receipt into his back pocket.

Alfie and Jo grabbed their things and followed Alfie's mum down to the bus stop on Albion Road to head to the museum. Alfie hoped it wouldn't take too long. Now which bus to take to the Museum stop?

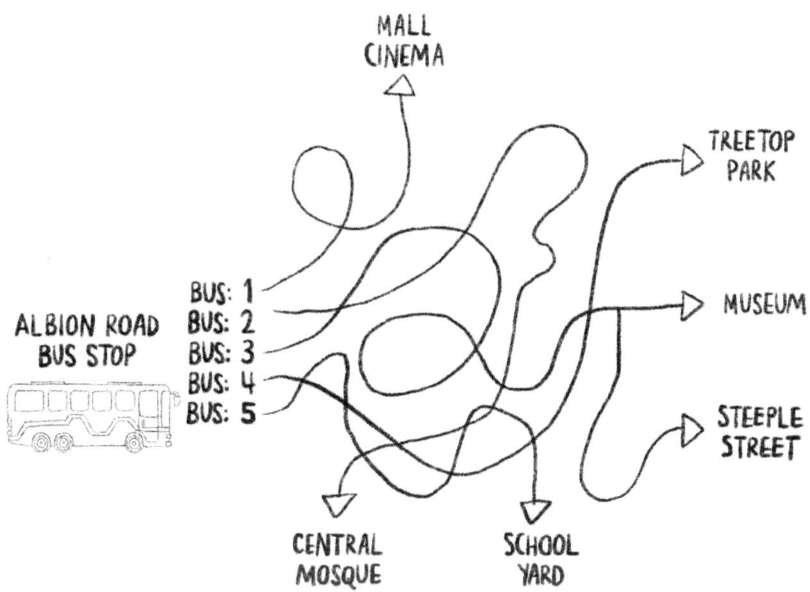

CHAPTER NINE

The trio jumped on the **number 3 bus**, which was about half full. There were adults with shopping bags stuffed with food, teenagers heading to the mall (playing terrible music really loudly on their phone), and right at the back a massive man with a leather jacket and a big beard, holding a tiny little sausage dog.

Alfie took a seat with Jo about half-way back, and his mum grabbed one in front. Time to watch the world go by. At one point a family walked past; a mum and dad holding the hands of a kid between them, who was being swung in the air squealing. An older brother was walking just behind sucking on a lolly pop and then running to catch up.

A little bit further up the road, a grey-haired couple were chatting as one pushed a buggy, with a toddler facing forward chewing on a carrot stick. Grandparents probably. Alfie wondered, what must it be like to have more family around than just your mum?

When they finally arrived at their stop, they stepped out of the bus and into the sun which reflected off the high white walls of the old museum. Inside was a sparkling marble floor, with large glass windows criss-crossing the ceiling. It felt much bigger than Alfie had expected. As he came through security, a giant of a guard checked all of their bags – although he didn't seem to look that hard.

'Right, I'm going to the café, you've got thirty minutes before we need to get the bus back, okay?' asked Alfie's mum looking at her watch.

'No problem, thanks Mum!' said Alfie, grabbing Jo's arm and following a sign to the right that led to the archives.

They pushed open two large white doors. Once inside Alfie gazed around the room in amazement at all the books, bags and boxes lining the walls; there must have been a thousand, or two thousand, items here. How many amazing stories from history must be on these shelves?

'Wow!' exclaimed Jo quietly, looking around.

But even after they checked this floor there would be more to see. One white spiral staircase headed to a floor above, while another rickety wooden set of steps headed down to what must have been a basement.

'Right, let's start on this floor first. We can split up and go each way around the shelves and meet in the middle,' said Alfie. 'I'll go this way.' He started off to the right before Jo called him back. 'Wait a minute Sherlock, what exactly are we looking for?' she asked.

'Well…' started Alfie. But, truthfully, he wasn't sure. He glanced along the first row of shelves. 'I guess we're looking for a label with the number on it, right?' said Alfie, taking the receipt back out. '1184' he read aloud.

But he could see immediately that the items weren't organised on shelves by number, but by type. The first row of shelves was labelled 'Sports,' the next set had the label, 'Tools'.

Jo was following him now, reading the labels alongside him. 'Where would a cup be? Aha, Kitchen Utensils!' she said, pointing at a row low down to their right. Each box had a label with the item, country, and number on it. They checked the label on each box, but none matched what they were looking for.

'It's not here!' said Alfie, disappointed.

'Well, I suppose a cup could fit in all sorts of places. It could be for drinking, but it could be a trophy, or for collecting water. Who knows?'

'We'd need to check every shelf to be sure,' said Alfie, looking around the enormous room.

'Let's look at each label and check for any that are from Egypt first. That would narrow it down more quickly,' he said to Jo.

'Okay, but we better be quick,' she paused as she looked at her watch, 'twenty-six minutes left!'

'Well, let's get going then!' exclaimed Alfie.

The two friends headed off in each direction. Alfie ran his eyes along each shelf, looking for the country name. If it didn't say Egypt, he knew he could move on. If it did, he'd check the item number.

It seemed to take forever, but finally he was heading towards Jo at the other side of the shelves.

'Anything?' asked Jo. Alfie shook his head. Jo looked

at her watch. 'Seven minutes left,' she said.

'Perhaps we do need to give up for today... there's just too many to check,' moaned Alfie, ready to admit defeat. But within a few seconds Jo pushed her shoulders back and took a big breath before saying, 'Nope, seven minutes is seven minutes. I'll go up, you go down.' Before he could argue, Jo had turned to move at a jog to the white staircase leading to the floor above. So, Alfie headed to the winding older staircase heading down.

Even looking down from the first step, he could see it was much darker in the basement, and there were hundreds more boxes lining the walls. He took each wooden step slowly:

Creak,

Creak,

Creak.

As he reached the bottom, he could see that these items looked older and more worn, some in strange shapes, wrapped in brown paper. He looked at the first shelf 'Miscellaneous' it said. What did that mean?

Just as he was about to start scanning the labels, Alfie spotted a desk with an old lady sitting behind it. She had white frizzy hair, and round pink glasses perched on the end of her nose. She wore a blue jacket that looked almost dusty. It was creased and wrinkled, like it had never been ironed.

He plucked up the courage to go over, and took a deep breath.

'What can I help you with dear?' the woman asked, without even looking up. Her voice was low and croaky. It was as if she hadn't spoken in years.

'I'm looking for something Egyptian. It must have come to the archives around 1945. But... well, I don't know exactly *what* it's for.' It sounded crazy to say it out loud.

'Alright dear,' she said slowly in her raspy voice, 'any clues?'

'Well it came from an archaeological dig and it's described as a 'cup'. But it might have something to do with... cats? Black cats, maybe even... magical cats,' he said, expecting her to laugh in his face.

She looked up now, staring straight at him over those tiny glasses. Her eyes were bright blue and younger than she seemed; full of life.

'Are you sure that's what you want?' she asked quietly.

He didn't quite know what she meant, but replied quickly, 'Yes, I'm sure. You see, something happened to me, and I...' then he paused. He wasn't quite ready to tell his story yet. Not to a stranger anyway.

But she seemed to understand how important it was and nodded before he continued.

'Head right to the back, young man. Left corner, second row. You'll find what you need there.' She looked back down as soon as she'd finished speaking and started tapping away on an ancient-looking typewriter sitting on the desk.

She seemed so sure where he needed to go... but

how?

Alfie followed the instructions and found a set of shelves with small boxes, around 10cms square. The sign on these shelves read 'Small Artefacts'. Aha, 'Small', that was on the receipt too.

Alfie walked quickly along the shelf, scanning each label. Finally 'Egypt' jumped out at him. The year: '1945'. The number: '1184'.

As he started to reach out for the small box, he heard a shout from behind him.

'Alfie! What are you doing down here, I've been looking for you, come on up right now!' It was his mum, calling from along the shelves behind him, with Jo standing sheepishly by her side.

'Just a second mum,' he called, 'I'll meet you up there'.

He looked around to check he was alone and a poster on the wall beside him caught his eye: '**DO NOT** remove artefacts under any circumstances,' it read.

He mouthed the word 'Sorry' in its direction, as he popped the little box into his bag. Running back along the shelves, he reached the old woman, who was still looking down at her work.

'I couldn't spot it,' he lied quietly as he ran past her.

'Of course not….' she replied. But as he glanced back, he could have sworn he saw a slight smile run across her lips.

She looked up briefly, 'We'll be here if you need us again Alfie Green,' she called, before returning to her book.

Alfie was about to ask how the old lady knew his name, but as he heard another call from above he knew he didn't have time. He practically flew back up the creaking steps and straight into his mum who was waiting just at the top.

'Quick,' she said, grabbing his arm and starting to drag him out of the room, through the large glass entrance and back onto the street. 'We'll miss our bus!'

As it was, the bus doors were just beginning to close as they reached the stop, and his mum wrapped her knuckles on the door to get the drivers attention. He let them on with a shake of his head.

Alfie sat with his bag clasped tightly on his lap through the entire journey. Jo didn't ask what he'd found. She knew better than to speak about it with Alfie's mum so close, but once they got home, they went straight to Alfie's room and shut the door. Alfie took the box out of his bag and carefully laid it on his Spiderman bed covers.

'Let me open it,' said Jo, reaching for the box.

'No, I'll do it,' replied Alfie.

'I'll play you for it?' smiled Jo taking out her hand. 'Rock, Paper, Scissors? Best of five!'

This was always her answer to everything. Who would win and get to open the box?

	JO	ALFIE
ROUND 1		
ROUND 2		
ROUND 3		
ROUND 4		
ROUND 5		

Hint:

Rock beats: Scissors

Paper beats: Rock

Scissors beats: paper

CHAPTER TEN

<u>'I win!' called Jo</u>, doing a little jig to celebrate.

She grabbed the box, ripped up the lid, and poured out the contents onto the bedspread. 'Is that gold?' she gasped as something small and shiny fell out of the box. It certainly looked gold at first sight. Before Alfie could pick it up, Jo's hand shot out and grabbed it. 'Nah, doesn't feel like metal,' she said, turning it over in her hand. 'It's too light'.

The sides of the little artefact were a few millimetres thick. And although the outside was gold, the inside was white.

'Well it wouldn't be a very useful cup. The bottom isn't flat enough to even put it down!' she said, running her fingers over the curved bottom of the small item. 'It's almost pointy.'

She turned it again. 'And it would cut your lips if you drank from the top – the edge is all rough. It's pottery I think. You feel it.'

Alfie leant in close to take it. 'I've seen something like this before somewhere. Wait a minute! This is the ear that's missing from the...' But before he could finish his sentence, his fingers made contact with the pottery ear and...

BOOM! WHOOSH!

Jo was thrown back on the bed and Alfie's mind was gone again.

He opened his eyes. Where was he this time?

He was back in the desert, but now he was outside, standing on the sand with the sun burning down on him.

He was leaning into the opening of the tomb where his great grandfather was presumably inside, and it looked pitch black down there.

A man was next to him, crouched on the floor, beginning to lower down a lamp. 'Look out below!' he called.

Alfie looked around himself, in every direction people were busy digging sand, moving boxes or setting up tents. As he stepped back, his foot hit something hard on the ground. Next to his feet was an old wooden door nestled in the sand. In the centre it had Egyptian characters carved into a neat rectangle. He leant in close to look at them. Five symbols. What could they mean? He looked at each one in turn and tried to commit them to memory.

Clink

A noise sounded below making him jump.

In his fright he dropped the ear back onto his bed spread and in an instant he had returned to the present. Alfie opened his eyes to find Jo sitting close in front of him staring straight at him, her mouth wide open.

'Are you okay? What happened? You looked like

you'd fallen asleep?' the questions came tumbling out.

'It was like before – like I stepped back in time,' explained Alfie. 'This time I was above the tomb, and there was something written on the tomb door. A message in hieroglyphs.'

'Can you remember them?' asked Jo urgently.

'I think so,' said Alfie, closing his eyes tight to picture what he saw. Jo grabbed him a piece of paper so he could sketch down the symbols he had seen, before they left his mind.

He frantically drew the images before pointing towards a book sitting on his bedside table. It was the one he'd picked up at the library. 'Grab that,' he said with urgency, before flicking it open to chapter four. Perhaps they could translate what he had seen?

Here's what Alfie saw:

Chapter 4: Hieroglyphs

Egyptians used symbols like letters to spell out many of their words, just like we do today. It's thought some words and phrases also had their own special symbol:

	Life		Death		Dance
	Guard		Pot		Rabbit
	Soldier		Cat		King
	Bull		Give		Take
	House		Do not		Water

CHAPTER ELEVEN

Alfie looked for each symbol in turn and wrote down the corresponding word beneath, before handing the paper to Jo:

<u>Cat Guard.</u>
<u>Do Not Take.</u>
<u>Death.</u>

Jo gasped, and looked at Alfie, confused. 'What does it mean?'

'I think it was a warning. The cat was guarding the tomb. And no one was meant to take it away,' explained Alfie. 'If you did take the cat then you would be punished by... death.'

'But they did take the cat,' exclaimed Jo, shocked. 'And we have its ear right here.' She pointed at the golden ear lying on the bed, now wishing they hadn't brought it home. Maybe it was dangerous; cursed even. 'What should we do with it?' she asked.

They sat quietly for several minutes, brains whirring. 'I've got it!' exclaimed Alfie. He jumped up like a jack-in-the-box. Now he knew what they needed to do. 'We need to reunite the ear with the cat statue. Maybe that will help her travel back to where she was meant to be.'

There was nothing for it. They'd have to sneak out yet again.

They cycled in silence before they approached the little run-down house for the second time that day. Nothing had followed them this time, and Alfie hoped that they were in for an easier arrival.

No such luck.

As they pulled up to the house, they could see more cats than ever. There must have been thirty or more that were lying down or sitting proudly upright in the garden. Some were alone, some in pairs or groups. Then, up on the roof, another twenty or so were clinging tightly to the tiles, looking down on them.

They didn't look like they'd spotted Jo and Alfie... yet. The duo lay their bikes as quietly as they could by the path. Carefully, Jo stepped forward:

CRACK!

With her first step she'd managed to crush a twig. In the silence it sounded like a bullet firing. The cats looked around as one. All eyes turned their way. Alfie looked towards the house, and in the doorway sat the largest black cat he had ever seen. Exactly like the one from his dream. It looked the pair up and down, then leapt forward screeching, her sharp claws bared in their direction.

'HISSSSS! SCREEECH!'

This seemed to be a call to arms for the other cats, who all stood up and moved slowly, very slowly, towards Alfie and Jo. Their bright eyes focused on the children as they moved closer.

'What should we do?' asked Jo, afraid, her voice trembling. Even she was scared today.

'I don't know...' replied Alfie, his mind spinning. He needed to do something. Soon the cats would reach them, and he didn't want to know what a thousand claws felt like.

'Unless.... maybe.... just maybe....' he murmured.

He took off his backpack and put it onto the floor. Carefully he reached inside and found the broken ear that he had wrapped in tissues from home. He unwrapped the artefact and laid it on his palm on the tissue paper, making sure he didn't touch it with his bare hand – this wouldn't be a good moment to go back in time!

He held it out towards the big black cat by the house, who seemed to be the leader. It stopped hissing immediately. The other cats stopped too and looked towards the large black moggy. Finally the largest cat moved away from the door. Following her lead, the other cats stepped back too. The path was now clear to get to the house. Carefully, Alfie and Jo walked up the path, and pushed at the open door.

Ray was sitting with his eyes closed and completely still in the armchair, the curtains closed at all the windows around him. Probably for the best. Seeing all those cats was terrifying.

'Excuse me,' said Jo quietly. He didn't stir. 'Excuse

me,' she said again, louder this time. Still he didn't move. Was he...?

'Sir?' called Jo, as politely but loudly as she could. Finally Ray opened his eyes and sat forward. Jo and Alfie sighed with relief.

'You came back!' he called, looking pleased. His eyes wrinkled even more as he smiled. 'What did you find out?' he asked.

'Well, Charlie is definitely my ancestor, you were right about that. And something we found in his old bag from Egypt led us to this...' Alfie opened his hand to show him the broken ear still tucked in the tissue paper in his palm.

'We think the cat wants it back!' jumped in Jo, keen to get going. It sounded crazy, but then nothing about today had been normal.

'What are you waiting for then?' Ray stood up, wobbly with excitement.

Alfie rushed into the old Finds Room. Inside it was quiet as night and dust hung in the air like stars. He walked through the boxes, jars and statues up to the black cat. Jo followed and let out a gasp as she saw it for the first time.

'So this is it. The cursed cat. It really is absolutely beautiful.' She was entranced by it. As she started to walk towards it, her arm reached out ahead of her, ready to feel it's cold surface.

'Don't touch!' shouted Alfie and Ray together. Jo pulled back her hand quickly and Alfie stepped in front of her. He moved towards the cat and leant down, so he was looking straight into its dark shining eyes. Then he spoke to the statue.

'I think you've been looking for this,' he whispered. 'I'm sorry my ancestor broke it. And that you were taken away. Maybe being put back together will help you find your way to your master in the afterlife?'

He looked at the shiny golden ear in his hand one last time, then finally took it with his bare hand to hold it up to the broken edge where it had snapped from all those years before.

A spark jumped from the cat, through the ear, and into Alfie's hand. The dust in the room swirled around them. Whirling up like a tornado around his legs, his body, his arms, and up to his face.

Then, suddenly the dust wasn't dust at all, but sand, reeling in circles, like flour in a mixer. Wind rushed in Alfie's ears…

BOOM! WHOOSH!

Then it stopped.

Silence...........

Alfie opened his eyes. It was dark. He stepped forward and heard crunching beneath his feet. It was familiar now. Warm sand. The air was musty again. He must be back down in the tomb.

He blinked hard, desperate that this time that he would get a proper look around. As his eyes grew accustomed to the dark, he could make out a man in a leather hat a few metres in front of him.

'Look out below!' came down that shout once again,

and Alfie looked up to see the lantern begin to descend towards him.

Alfie moved forward a few steps towards the man in the hat. He recognised him now. It was definitely the same man from the old photo. It was his great grandfather, Charlie Green.

The lantern came closer and closer, wobbling on the end of the rope. Alfie watched, almost in slow motion, as the lamp hit the cat and a tiny 'clink' rang out. The cat's ear fell silently, landing right inside his great grandfather's discarded bag, which lay open at his feet. This must have been how it had ended up coming back with his things!

Finally the lantern came close enough for his great grandfather to catch it.

Now, in the light, Alfie could see the cat statue where it should be. Not hidden away in a house in England, but sitting proudly, guarding whoever's tomb this had once been. It looked strong and powerful here. Not out of place, as it looked at Ray's house. It should never have been moved when it was found. The symbols on the door had warned anyone who entered. But they hadn't listened.

His great grandfather tutted and looked to the ground to see the broken ear. Then he moved the lantern to get a closer look at the cat. He reached out a hand to touch the jagged edge of the break. Alfie knew what would happen if he didn't do something. The curse would come true. His grandfather would disappear. Peter Murrey would take the cat to England, and the ear would be lost into the archives.

This is why the cat had sent him here. The artefacts needed to stay exactly where they were. Where they were meant to be.

Before he could think, Alfie heard his own voice calling loudly, more loudly than he'd ever shouted before:

'DON'T TOUCH!'

His great grandfather's head spun around, his eyes widening as he spotted a young boy calling out to him from the shadows. They locked eyes for just a second.

'THE CAT MUST STAY HERE!'

Alfie called out, willing his great grandfather to understand.
Charlie Green pulled his hand back from the cat with a nod.
Then...

BANG!

It was as if Alfie was falling down a hole, the walls flashing around him. Something was calling him back. If he squinted just a little, he could see it. Those familiar eyes...

Hint: this optical illusion works best if you squint your eyes and lean the page back and forth or side to side. Can you spot what appears?!

CHAPTER TWELVE

The **cat** had led him back to the present and there it was, that face once again. Finally Alfie could open his eyes. He had returned to the Finds Room at Ray's house. His hand was still outstretched, but the cat he had been reaching for had gone. And in his hand, where the ear had been, was nothing at all. It was empty.

He looked around himself. The room that had been so dusty and jam packed with artefacts was now a warm snug, with two large armchairs against the back wall, a bright checked rug in the centre, and a display cabinet with a selection of just a few well-looked-after items from the past. A jug here, a selection of old coins there.

Then he heard a noise behind him. Jo was entering the room.

'You alright in here?' she asked brightly. 'That was a big bang!'

'I did it, Jo! I found him and called out and it worked, he heard me, I'm sure of it!' he put up his hand to high five Jo, but she just looked at him bemused.

'What on earth are you talking about?!' she laughed. 'Come on, we better get home, you don't want your mum to worry,' she rolled her eyes and turned to head out through the door. Alfie followed, not sure what to think. It was like Jo had forgotten everything that had happened...

As he walked back through the hall, he turned into the front room. He could see this too looked lighter and brighter than it had before. The TV was playing quietly in the corner and on the table were three plates with cake crumbs scattered across them, two half-drunk glasses of juice, and a cup of tea.

'Hello?' Alfie called out into the room. For a second he thought it was empty, and then he heard a jolly voice, round and deep - 'Ello'. He turned further into the room, and there was Ray, smart in a neatly ironed shirt and trousers. His grey hair was combed, his face clean shaven so his rosy cheeks could be clearly seen. He had a wide smile across his face, like he was... happy.

'You found the loo okay then boy?' he asked, before standing up and walking towards the doorway. 'So nice of you two young'uns to stay for tea, but it really wasn't necessary. Anyone would have helped you out in my position. I'm just glad your leg is okay.' He pointed to Jo's leg, which she twisted around in circles and said, 'Yeah, definitely not broken, I'll just need to rest it I reckon.' She smiled and started to walk out of the room and down the hall. Alfie followed in a daze.

Once they reached the door, Jo turned around and called, 'Thanks again Ray.'

'Well, goodbye, safe cycle home,' he replied, ushering the two gently out of the door. Alfie's mouth opened and shut, but no words came out. He followed Jo outside, where the sun was shining down on them bright and warm, and birds were singing in the hedgerows. It was like a cloud had lifted from around them. From around the house.

'Wow, lovely weather for cycling. Let's go home,' smiled Jo turning back to Alfie. She grabbed her bike from the path. 'Maybe you'll beat me for the first time with this leg!' she laughed, climbing on her bike.

Alfie picked up his own bike, but before he followed he turned back to take one more look up at the old house. It looked the same, but also like everything had changed.

Alfie jumped on his bike and rode hard to catch up. Then, quietly the two friends cycled home. Alfie dropped Jo back at her house first, before he headed to his own home.

Alfie propped his bike up against the garden wall and walked towards his front door, relieved to be back. Then he stopped. A noise beside him made him look down, a small 'meow'. At his foot was a black kitten, fur glossy, eyes a shiny green. It rubbed up against Alfie's leg happily, and he reached down to stroke it, making the animal purr.

'Oh thank goodness! Where have you been?' exclaimed his mum opening the door and calling down the path, her face creased with worry. 'I was just about to start calling around!'

She beckoned him in, and as he took his hand away from the cat, it walked calmly down the path out into the sunshine, with a quick look back at him before turning around the corner and disappearing.

'I'm absolutely fine Mum. Trust me,' he replied, heading inside and collapsing onto the sofa in his living room. 'I had a weird day. Really weird. But maybe the most exciting day I've EVER had.'

'Ooohh, what were you doing?' replied his mum with relief, following close behind and sitting back into the armchair opposite.

'Just our… homework,' replied Alfie, not sure she'd want to know exactly what went on.

'Your homework?' asked his mum, crossing her arms and raising her eyebrows, looking extremely puzzled.

'Yes, you know, the history project I told you about. The one about my great grandfather, Charlie Green,' said Alfie quietly. Well, it wasn't a complete lie.

'Great Grandfather Green? I didn't know you were interested in him,' said his mum coming to sit next to him. It was like she didn't remember getting the box down earlier, or their conversation about his great grandfather just hours before. Had everyone forgotten what had happened but him?

'He was a lovely old guy; you would have liked him I think. And his stories!' she smiled warmly.

'You met him?' he asked, surprised. 'I thought you said you hadn't. He disappeared out in Egypt, didn't he?' he said.

'What?' she laughed, 'well I don't know where you got that from!' She put an arm around him. 'He lived to a ripe old age. Although, you know he did go to Egypt a couple of times, so you're right about that. He was into old stuff when he was a young man. But he was no good at it, he never found a thing!

'I think your father said he gave that all up quite suddenly and came home to settle down with your great gran gran. He became a teacher or something.'

Alfie couldn't believe his ears.

'I've got a few photos of him if you want them for your project. Just as an old man I'm afraid.' His mum got up and went to the large shelf of photo albums above the books. She ran her hand along them, took down an old album and began flicking through.

She brought the album over and Alfie leant in to look. There was a group of men, grey and wrinkly. Like a gang of old friends. In the centre was one old man with a small boy sitting on his lap. The man was greyer than he'd been before, but Alfie could still recognise him as the person he'd seen back in the tomb with the statue. It was definitely his great grandfather, Charlie Green, alive and well. 'There he is. He must be in his seventies here I think,' said his mum pointing at the central man.

Alfie's mum laid the album on his lap and busied herself looking for more photos in a box. Alfie took the chance to reach into his pocket and pull out the small old photo he'd taken from Ray's house. He looked around the group in the album. And there, right next to his great grandad, was a face he recognised, still with his black hat on his head. Older of course, but here was Charlie's friend from the tomb door. Their friendship had survived after all.

'Who's the boy on his lap?' asked Alfie leaning in closer to see a small child on his great grandfather's knee.

His mother paused and took a deep breath, 'That's your father.'

Alfie felt his heart skip. He'd never seen a baby photo of his dad. He was smiling up at his great grandad.

He looked happy.

His mum was standing now at the bookcase, her arm reaching to the back of the shelf. 'Now what's this?' she said quietly as she pulled down another large black photo album. 'Gosh, I'd forgotten I'd put this up here!' she said, rubbing her hand over the cover, dust falling to the carpet below. 'Perhaps it's time we open this back up,' she murmured, before returning to where Alfie was sitting.

'Alfie, do you want to see some more photos of your father? It's your choice,' she asked. Her voice sounded uncertain.

'Of course!' replied Alfie, a big smile spreading across his face.

His mum returned the smile with relief and sat back down to lay the album between them. It fell open on a picture of Alfie's mum holding a wobbly looking birthday cake in front of his dad, with a very young Alfie on his dad's lap. All three were leaning their heads back and laughing.

Alfie's mum smiled to see the picture again after so long. 'Oh that was a lovely day… it was your first birthday and we'd been up since 5am because your dad was so excited about you opening your presents!' She paused before speaking again. 'You won't remember of course, but he got you this big old globe. You used to spin it around and around,' she laughed. 'He said he wanted you to travel the world when you grew up, just like he did. He loved his adventures you know. Perhaps he got that from your great grandad and his travels as a young man?' She smiled. 'And soon it'll be your birthday again,

Alfie.'

'Yep – eleven this year mum,' said Alfie, still looking at the photo.

'I guess you really are growing up,' came his mum's voice, quieter this time. He looked up to see her looking at him closely.

Alfie turned the pages of the book, looking closely at each image of his father. Outside their new house, another birthday, at the zoo. It was amazing how objects, photos, and stories can connect you to your past. But Alfie wished he knew more about his dad's life. And his death.

'What are you thinking about?' asked his mum.

'I just wondered if… if you could tell me about Dad, how he… died,' he asked quietly, looking back at the album.

'Well,' his mum paused. 'We don't really know. One minute he was there, the next he wasn't.' Alfie's ears pricked up, like a dog when a whistle sounds.

'So, he just disappeared?' he asked, looking up at her now.

'I guess you could say that,' she took a deep breath. 'We were out hill walking, up on holiday in Scotland. It was cold and drizzly, and we were walking through some neolithic building remains right above the sea. There were low walls, deep holes and high burial mounds. All the remains of a village that people would have lived in thousands of years ago. It was fascinating,' she smiled remembering how the day had begun.

'And then I heard a loud crack, no a **boom** almost,

from where your father was behind me. When I looked back… he was gone.' Alfie's heart began to race.

'We looked of course. For days we looked. Me, the local people, even the police. But there were so many high edges around the area we'd been exploring. Sheer cliffs down into the lake below. We didn't even find where he'd slipped, nothing was disturbed, no skids in the mud, or knocked stones…' her voice trailed off. 'But he was doing what we loved, having an adventure. Accidents happen.' Her voice was almost a whisper now.

'If it was an accident?' asked Alfie quietly, more to himself than anyone else.

'Pardon?' his mum asked, her eyebrows furrowed.

'Nothing,' Alfie shook his head. He didn't want to upset her. But since his own journey to the past, and seeing his great grandfather's disappearance, he felt like almost anything could be possible.

He wondered, was there any chance the same thing had happened to his dad? Maybe he had touched something and…. **BOOM! WHOOSH!**… he'd disappeared? One minute he was there, the next he was gone, just like his mum said.

And if his grandad had come back, maybe his dad could too. Was there a way Alfie could find him? Perhaps not today, or tomorrow, but maybe something in the future might lead Alfie to him. Just as the cat had led him to his great grandad.

'Aha, now that must be one of my favourite photos ever!' Alfie's mum's voice brought him back from his thoughts. She was pointing at a Polaroid photo of Alfie and both his parents sitting in the park having a picnic.

Alfie was only two at the time, but as he looked at the photo the moment began to creep back to him. The sweet taste of the strawberries, a little warm from the walk, the sound of the stream nearby while they ate, and that familiar smell of his dad. The memory felt like a word on the tip of his tongue.

He took a deep breath and leant in close to the smiling photo. 'I think I remember this too, Mum. I guess everyone has important memories that stay with them...'

Hint: what's an important memory for you? You can write down your memory or draw it in a 'photo frame'.

CHAPTER THIRTEEN

ONE MONTH LATER

It was the first week of summer holidays and Alfie was looking forward to long hot days with nothing to do.

Since his big adventure, things had changed around the house. His mum seemed to be really, really trying not to nag him quite so much, or to warn him about every possible danger that might be around the corner. Although he could see in her eyes she still wanted to.

There hadn't been one mysterious cat in his life this month. Not one. And he was beginning to like it that way. In fact, the best thing that had happened was they'd got… not a cat… but a… dog!

His mum had spotted him at the rescue centre when she'd passed the window on her way to work. Every day the scruffy little dog had been there looking out at her. She just couldn't resist. Apparently he was also going to 'teach Alfie about responsibility', so she said…

Alfie didn't know about that, but he did know he loved having another person, well animal, around at home.

Roger (that was what they'd called him) was a

caramel-coloured ball of fur. A 'Mutt' someone said, and perhaps he was. But he was great. Always a bit muddy and often a bit smelly, but he had become part of the family very quickly. He gave Alfie the perfect excuse to get out of the house too. His mum seemed not to worry so much if he had Roger with him.

'I'm taking Roger out for a walk mum; I won't be long!' he called, this particular sunny day with nothing to do and nowhere to be.

'Here boy,' Alfie called to where Roger was lying in a pile by the sofa in his snuggly bed. The little dog immediately jumped up and ran over to him with his tail wagging. As they stepped outside and slammed the door, Alfie clipped on Roger's lead, and they started walking. Well rather, Roger started pulling Alfie along, who jogged to keep up.

They headed along Albion Road, then down past Jo's house, and further on to the parade of shops near the station. He suddenly felt a little hungry and was desperate for some of his favourite super sour sweets. He felt in his pocket and found a pound coin; 'Yes!' he murmured, before walking across the road.

On the other side, Roger stopped for a wee against a road sign. Alfie looked at the sign and read 'Holly Tree Road'. But it wasn't easy to read, as in the middle of the words there were three long grooves, deep and dark. They looked almost like scratch marks. Weird.

Roger sniffed up at the scratches and immediately flew backwards. He barked loudly and looked around himself. 'Calm down boy,' said Alfie, pulling him back and stroking his soft head. 'What's the matter?' Roger began to pull at the lead, drawing Alfie away from the sign. Something had definitely spooked him.

As they headed further along the road, Alfie realised that it didn't look quite like normal. It was almost like a ghost town. No kids on bikes, no cars in driveways, not even one person gardening in the neat patches of grass outside the houses. That was weird too.

He and Roger carried on walking towards the shop. Finally some life. There was a large white van outside, with the back doors open revealing it was full of boxes. Then Mr Fitz, the shop owner, who Alfie's mum always chatted with on a Friday when they picked up sweets, came rushing out of the shop with another box. It was piled high with pots and pans.

Alfie continued towards the shop door.

'Stop!' called Mr Fitz from behind him. Alfie turned, to see the shop owner staring at him, wide eyed and trembling. 'We're closed!' he called out.

'What's going on?' asked Alfie.

'You don't want to know son, just get out of here,' he replied.

'What do you mean?' asked Alfie, intrigued now.

'Look, I don't want to scare you, son. But, last night that.... **THING**… it was back.'

'What thing?' asked Alfie.

'The …. the creature. Haven't you heard?' He raised his eyebrows in surprise. 'It was all over the news!' he continued, 'and last night….' His voice drifted off and he shook his head. Ha! The news? Alfie did all he could to avoid watching that. It was always so boring.

The shop keeper spoke again, his voice cracking with fear: 'The first time it came, it destroyed our car bonnet. Left a massive dent across the top, and scratched it up with its claws. That was bad enough. But last night it shattered the windows at the front of the flat. And not just ours, all along the street!' Alfie looked up and down the street, and he could spot several houses with cardboard or wood covering smashed windows.

'What sort of *creature* is it?' asked Alfie.

'Who knows? Mrs Reed down the road thought she saw it running away in the early hours. She didn't get a great look at it. But it was big, and fast, and grey.'

'Like a big dog do you mean?' asked Alfie.

'Maybe. But do dogs have red eyes?' the man responded; his own eyes wide with terror. 'I dread to think what'll happen if it comes back tonight. That's why we're all getting out of here. And you should too! Get home son, and don't come back down this way again.' As soon as he said that, Roger tugged on the lead and sent Alfie flying.

The brave little dog pulled him back up the street and away from the shops, barking as he went. It seemed like he was trying to take Alfie back to safety.

As they passed by the road sign again, Alfie couldn't help but look at those marks across the name. They really did look like claw marks. He reached over to run a finger along the deep cut and...

BOOM! WHOOSH!

He was somewhere else.

It had happened again.

Last time he'd ended up in an Egyptian tomb; where would he go today?

He opened his eyes, and looked around.

There were trees, fields of grass, a lake far in the distance. Not so strange… but… there was no town, or road or cars. He could feel pebbles of a path beneath his feet, and in the distance was a row of small wooden houses, smoke rising up from one where a chimney stood proud on the roof.

The world sure did look different. But more importantly he felt different. Bigger. Heavier. Hairier.

It was almost like he was looking out from someone else's eyes.

Or something else.

He tried to speak out, but he couldn't hear a voice, just a growl. And in response he heard a noise in the distance. A long, deep howl.

AAAAAAAA ROOOOOOOOOOOOOOOOOO!

Then Roger must have pulled Alfie back from the sign, because as his hand dropped, he was back in the present, looking at the road sign with those deep, dark marks. Within seconds, they were racing back along the street, Roger dragging them home. As they ran, letters whirled around Alfie's mind, flicking through his brain like a ball bouncing off the walls. But it made no sense. What was his mind trying to tell him?

Wait a minute! Was that a word that he was starting to see? Yes. There it was....

Hint: unscramble the letters to find the hidden word!

PROLOGUE

<u>WEREWOLVES</u>.

Was that where he had gone? Into the mind of a....
Werewolf? That would be crazy though, wouldn't it?

He could feel another adventure beginning...

THE END

Or is it....?

CONGRATULATIONS

You've helped Alfie and Jo solve their first mystery. But it's not the end.

Look out for the second Time Riddler's adventure coming soon!

If you enjoyed this book, please add a review on your favourite book-buying website to help more kids find this brand-new history mystery series.

To find out more about how this book was written by mother and son writing duo, Holly and Gus, visit: www.hollygreenland.com/books

CROSSWORD ANSWERS

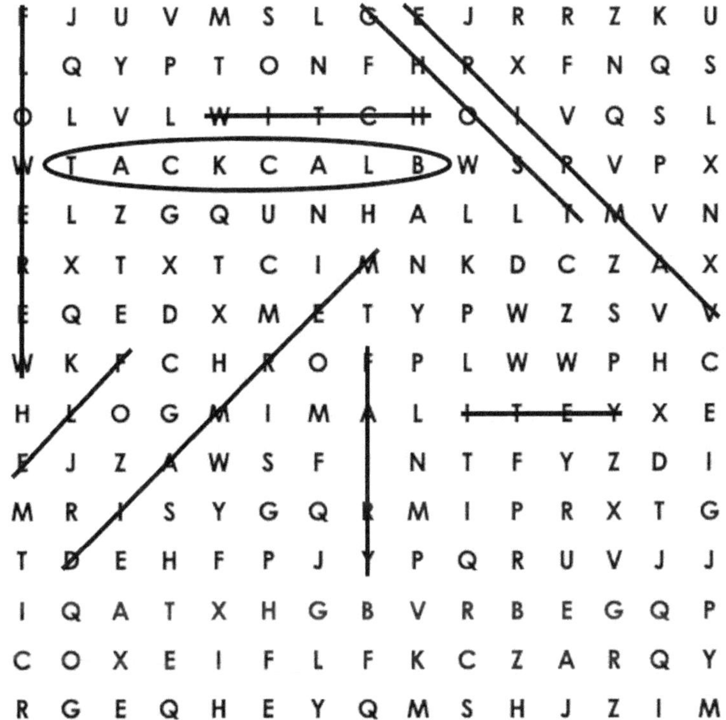

ABOUT THE AUTHORS

Holly and Gus are a mum and son writing duo based just outside London, in the UK. They came up with the idea for the Time Riddlers series in lockdown 2020.

Scaredy Cat was inspired by Gus's love of history, myths and scary stories. They have lots of new adventures for Alfie and Jo planned, so keep your eyes open!

www.hollygreenland.com/books